Ruth, whose name in Hebrew means 'Beautiful', did not seem to have success on her side. There had been three deaths in her household, she was poverty stricken and had to begin a new life, in a new land, gleaning alien corn. Yet, this unknown Moabitess through marriage became one of the most outstanding women in the world's history, in literature, and in God's eternal plan. Through her Royal Household was born the Saviour of the world. In this book the author traces her amazing story and tries to draw a few lessons for people, everywhere.

RUTH

RUTH

A LOVE STORY
WITH SECRETS FOR LIVING

DERICK BINGHAM

MBASSADOR

ISBN 0 907927 76 9

AMBASSADOR PRODUCTIONS LTD.
Providence House,
16 Hillview Avenue,
Belfast, BT5 6JR, UK.

Dedicated to my mother
Ruth

Contents

DERICK BINGHAM has a reputation for delivering a profound message with sharp wit, piercing logic, and complete honesty, he has authored a number of books, including the best-sellers *Promises To Keep* and *The Edge of Despair* and is also a columnist with the *Christian Herald*. Derick is a Bible Teacher with the Crescent Church, Belfast. Audio and Video recordings of his ministry reach out across the country and overseas.

Introduction

Suddenly, in the midst of a busy day a letter drops onto your doormat. It proves to be a love letter. It is private. It says things to you that transcends the hectic traffic outside. You are transported out of the mundane nitty-gritty everyday routine by a warm, loving, inspiring feeling. You have received more than a letter: you have been delivered a message to your heart which has made your day and the rest of your life, perhaps, different.

The message from Ruth in the Bible is like that. It lies between the warring, murdering, scheming stories of the Book of Judges and often frightening turbulent days which are recorded in the two books of Samuel. It is a love story. Yet it is more than just a story of a romance between a desperately poor girl and a very wealthy land owner: it is a story of love for God, of love for His people and all that they believe.

I wrote this little book just after the death of my mother. I wrote it in just one week staying quietly by the sea at Clifden in Conemmara, at the Abbeyglen Hotel near where Alcock and Brown landed after the first epic Trans-Atlantic flight from America to the continent of Europe. I was 22 and was extremely naive and inexperienced in many areas of life but the comfort and calm, inspiration and guidance I received in my young heart from this biblical love story was an experience I will never forget.

The story begins with a tragedy, but then out of the womb of all tragedy there comes something beautiful, which if the tragedy had never occurred, would never have been seen. Great pleasure has been experienced by countless millions of people as a result of the lessons learned from the pain of Ruth's story. Facing tragedy, loneliness and poverty Ruth allowed God to have His way in her life and accepted the rough with the smooth as the matchless Divine Potter slowly moulded her into the person He wanted her to be. Come, let us walk together through those long ago days in Israel, as John Keats would have put it, 'Amidst alien corn.' The message of Ruth is ultimately very simple: God always goes where He is wanted.

Derick Bingham
Belfast 1992

1

'Till Loneliness And Death Step Up To Greet Me'

"Duties our ours, events are the Lords"
- Samuel Rutherford

Loneliness hurts and it can come in the strangest places. I can think of two places it hurt me.

It was a beautiful hot August afternoon and we were in New York City to preach about the Lord Jesus. Having no engagements that afternoon I took myself to the centre of the city and walked the length of Fifth Avenue from West Fifty-seventh Street corner to Times Square and back. Thousands upon thousands of people were on the street, laughing, talking and jostling. Young girls with their leather shoulder bags swinging along; smooth American businessmen with great knotted neck ties; small suntanned children charging

here, there and yonder. Saks, Tiffanys, and all
the rest were drawing their customers. I had
dreamed of this place, but as I stood watching
it all I felt about as lonely as if I were on the
top of Slieve Donard in Ulster with the wind
tugging my coat. Alone in a strange land!

Strange things may fascinate, but when you
are alone in facing them: loneliness can sting.
You know what I mean. You are taken into a
crowded room and are introduced to the 'in'
set. They smile at you, say the right thing and
then turn to each other and go right on where
they left off. In the end you busy yourself
reading the words on a record sleeve or
something just as irrelevant in order to cover
the loneliness you feel. You have not got the
right school tie on or don't drive the proper
make of car; so you don't make it.

There is a beautiful little phrase used by the
ever-gentle Amy Carmichael which sums up
the answer to loneliness in a strange land.
Talking of India and the most complicated
work of trying to save girls from child pros-
titution and the snake of the subsequent evils
she wrote:

"It was in gentle, generous, patient ways
like this that we learned not to fear any

strangeland. Even if He is the only one whom we know there, He is enough".

He is enough? We were far away from Fifth Avenue as the train rocketed on into the night. Five of us, all college students, were in our bunks on the edge of dream.

I could hear the boys breathing heavily and dropping off to sleep one by one. For me it simply would not come. I tried them all - counting sheep, jumping a gate, telling my toes to settle and relax, then my legs, then my whole body. It was useless because my sheep got stuck in the bars of the gate and nearly broke their necks, and my toes were in an unsettled mood.

I threw back the small curtain of the train window and gazed out as the small Russian villages seemingly swam past. A thousand miles from home, in a very strange land, coupled with an ominous feeling regarding the Communist regime that surrounded me did not make me feel uplifted. Alone in a strange land!

The Bible lay on the bunk and reaching over I opened it. The ancient words stared up at me and thrilled my very soul: "My peace I give unto you, not as the world giveth give I unto you . . . Let not your heart be troubled, neither let it be afraid". I had Him, and He was enough. I was asleep in two minutes.

Ruth, the Moabitess was lonely because of death. Widowhood for this beautiful girl had come early in life and, believe me, it was as real to her as to a Jacqueline Kennedy or a Coretta King. Death to most people, until it comes to their own door, is distant. People are sorry, yes, but do not remain sorrowful. Tears do not seem to flow when death is down the road. Let it take a mother, a father, a brother or a sister from your house and you'll know all about the empty room, the missing voice, the vacuum that will never again be filled. You never get over missing them: you just have to get used to living without them. It was no different three thousand years ago.

But not only one death had come to Ruth's door. There were two more. Chilion, her husband, Mahlon, her brother-in-law, and Elimelech, her father-in-law. Three males out of one house is a strange occurrence. The details are not given as to the causes of death, but it would seem that the death of Ruth's husband in particular had come early in her married life because there is no record of any children. Then, to add to it all, there was a famine in the land. In Ireland we know only too well what that can mean. The very place in which these words are being written on the Connemara coast was ravaged by famine a few decades ago and thousands perished. The old folk can tell you stories to this day. Hunger, death and loneliness all stepping up to greet you does not exactly make a success story.

That, of course, is the very kind of situation in which God works. With us there is a difficulty in every opportunity, but with Him there is an opportunity in every difficulty. Watch now, as God begins to work in the storm tossed life of the Moabitess lass. There are lessons to be learned here which if you can learn now, will save you countless heartbreaks later.

In the Bible story of Ruth over fifty out of a total of eighty-five verses are taken up with dialogue, so it is obvious that the writer (probably Samuel) prefers to tell his story through conversations. The first series of conversations occurring after the tragedy and at the time of famine are primarily taken up with reaction to the situation. Reaction to situations has a bigger part to play in life than we can ever imagine. Your reaction to trouble, when it comes, steers the ship of life through the storm to the harbour or onto the rocks. Watch as God records their reactions. Her mother-in-law's reaction comes first, her sister-in-law's second, and Ruth's third.

Naomi, the Bible indicates, was the first to move. "Then she arose with her daughters-in-law that she might return from the country of Moab; for she had heard in the country of Moab how that the Lord had visited His people in giving them bread". That she should not have moved away in the first place, most theologians are agreed. Elimelech, her husband, had maybe more to do with it than she. Her name means "Pleasure" but when she eventually got home to Bethlehem she said, "Call me not Naomi, call me Mara . . . (Bitterness) . . . I went out full, and the Lord hath brought me home again empty". She was, like many another, far away from the Lord. Like you, maybe. Once close, happy, nothing between you and the Saviour you had trusted. Your Bible was your delight, Christian fellowship was your companionship, prayer was your very spiritual breath. Now you are cold, critical, and miserable. Spiritual things you keep up outwardly, mechanically even, to make a show because you have an old reputation to keep. Your heart is far from Him. You did not even bend your knees today to the One who thought it worthwhile to shed His blood for you at Calvary. You are neither happy "in the world" or "in the church". you are neither hot nor cold. Don't worry, I've been there many times. As dead as the letter of the law. All talk and no power. All truth and no burning love for the Lord Jesus. Famine in your soul, filled with loneliness in that you no longer have His close companionship, and experiencing spiritual death in your effectiveness for God.

But "she arose". She knew what was wrong. She knew where the answer lay. God had not run away, she had. She "went out full"; have you? Money and affluence have deadened your zeal. Things matter more than God. Maybe the Lord is bringing you back empty to give you Himself again. It reminds me of my friend, James Barton. He told me how he was sickened by the material grabbing Christians in the West. He has given his life to working for the spreading of the Gospel in India and he told me of how much the spirit of materialism hurt his soul. At his gate, opening onto a street, there lives a family. They actually live on the street. The little boys go to school from there and return there at night. No roof over their heads, just a little corner at Jimmy's gate. Can you imagine my friend's reaction when his own little boy asked his dad could he give his worn-out jeans to his little friend at the gate. Shame on us and our grumblings. Maybe it would be good for us to be stripped to find that His grace is sufficient for us. Arise and go back to Him now. Go to your knees this very moment. The Lord has not moved away. His love is absolutely unchanging. He loves you still.

Orpah, which means "stiffnecked" comes next. Her reaction was understandable, but came so near the pathway of success that it is one of the saddest points in the story. Her husband was gone; her father-in-law had died and now she accompanies Naomi to the border of His land. She is counselled by Naomi to return to "her people" and "her gods". Let us not be too quick to blame Orpah. Obedience is not a virtue either to be overlooked or censured. She kissed her mother-in-law and returned to Moab.

"To kiss" and "to cling" nevertheless, are two very different reactions. They both speak volumes. Proximity does not mean affinity, and a kiss can even be casual. The words "but Ruth clung to her" made all the difference in the world. Ruth could not go; her woman-heart clung on. She did not kiss: she clung ! She tells Naomi of her great pledge. She wants to go where she goes, live where she lives. Naomi's people are to become her people and most important of all, Naomi's God is to be hers. She even wants to lie in the same grave.

If you and I had happened, by chance, to come walking past these two women we would probably have walked on. Just two women talking by the side of the road; the wind blowing up dust as usual, the sun pouring down on the quiet countryside at the time of barley harvest.

Yet, things are never as they seem. In the heart of that beautiful girl there struggled the biggest decision in her young life. She had discovered the true God and was she going to go back to the worldly substitutes in Moab that never satisfy? The loneliness of an alien land, the future seemingly blank, with little chance of gaining a husband, or the ease of familiar things? It's the old and endless question. God calls, we hear and . . .?

It came to a young sophisticated prince in the courts of Pharaoh; an alien wilderness with a load of grumblers or his social whirl? What was it to be? It was a lonely decision and very few people noticed when he made it- even those who were supposed to be on his side were against him. Did he lose? Forty-six years later. with the Red Sea, through which he led over a million people, the wilderness, and all the many miracles behind him, God takes a body and buries it on Mount Nebo. The body? That of the greatest leader of men history has ever seen. The meekest man in all the earth. He did not look it when he walked out of the palace that day.

Abram was called out to an alien land. He probably looked rather naive that day when he headed out of Ur of the Chaldees. He never dreamt that he was to father a great nation which Hitler's third Reich, Egypt's Nasser, or Russia herself could not break. But he believed God and it was accounted unto him for righteousness. He staggered not.

Miserable teenager! Scruff! Idiot! Running

down a valley with a stone on a sling against a man with a spear the size of a telegraph pole; never talk about his size. "What are you doing, David? He will give your flesh for the birds to eat". "The Lord of Hosts, I believe in Him". "Yes, so do I, but aren't you a little bold for your age? I mean, why draw the criticism of older and wiser men than you?" "The giant has defied the Lord and sitting around talking or arguing about the best way to bring him down won't do him any harm. I'm going to do something about it; let me go at him in the name of the Lord of Hosts".

The teenager made the decision himself and as far as I can see there was not a single man in all Israel who agreed with him, good, godly and right though they may have been; except the Lord. THAT made all the difference and lo, the giant came tumbling down. He looked stupid at the time but he became king afterwards.

It is always so! A young man here, a girl there, gets directions from the Lord for their life's work. Nobody pats them on the back. or rings them up on the phone to congratulate them when they decide to follow it. No Nobel prize comes their way. "Israel" sits back and watches how they will fare. If they are blessed, that is good; if they fail, we knew they would anyway.

The Lord, however, still lives in His heaven and His ways are not the ways of men. He noticed the heart of the girl and her decision as she stood on the road that day. He knew she was seeking His comfort and guidance. Nobody who ever reached out for that comfort and guidance was ever disappointed. It is the set of the sails and not the gales that tell us the way to go. Ruth's sails were set.

Who packed thy wallet, friend?
One whose love shall never end -
What therein was laid?
He put in bread and wine and stayed.
What said He thereon?
"Wilt thou want more than these when thou
art gone?"
How didst thou answer Him?
I begged a candle, for mine eyes were dim.
He bent on me His gaze
Clearer than a thousand days,
"Thou shalt need no light by any day or
night".
Then said I, "My fear

Was of a blackness when no hand was
near".
But He this word let fall:
"I shall not leave thee when thou leavest
all".
And wilt thou take a staff?
Of His cross He gave me half.
What shall be thy dress?
He clothed me in emptiness.
Dost thou need no book?
His face is all whereon I crave to look.
Hast thou no map or chart?
I know my road, it leadeth to His heart.

2

Amidst Alien Corn

"Give me the love that leads the way,
The faith that nothing can dismay,
The hope no disappointment hire,
The passion that will burn like fire.
Let me not sink to be a clod -
Make me Thy fuel, flame of God"

So, out of the blue there comes showers of blessing - Ruth finds wealth, happiness, and her man? Not so fast. God is never in any hurry. To find and do God's will is not accomplished all in the one day. He spent forty years training Moses after he yielded to His will. David fought a lion and a bear before he faced Goliath. Amos was first a shepherd in Tekoa. John lived in the wilderness. Peter had to learn his own weaknesses in the judgment hall before he led three thousand to his Lord at Pentecost. Paul first went to Arabia before he went to Jerusalem.

When you are under God's training the hardest lesson of all is to wait for Him. Work for Him, pray to Him, read about Him but, to wait for Him, there is the rub.

"They that wait upon the Lord shall renew their strength . . . They shall reap and not faint."

To find the will of God for one's life is probably the most difficult task in Christian existence. To search for it is not to degenerate into the merely interesting, the pretty. There is blood and iron in it. How am I to know? To the right or to the left? This job or that? Can I know, now? I always wanted to. To know, now; a voice out of the sky whispering, "go here, now there". But it just doesn't work that way.

The greatest guiding line to follow when faced with a decision as a Christian, I have found, is to shut your door. Get the influences of life out of the way and explain every-thing in secret to your heavenly Father. Acknowledge Him. Then go and act in a common sense manner according to your abilities and limitations. When you acknowledge Him He then directs your paths. Ask two simple questions, Is it right? and, Is it necessary? If there is no cloud between you and your Lord, go ahead. There is a word they use in the Far East for the phrase Paul wrote when he explained God's will as "Good . . . acceptable . . . and perfect". They say it should be that "Good and perfect and lovable will of God". If you submit, acknowledge and then act, you will find it will become not always pleasurable, but eventually lovable.

Such was the case with my heroine, Ruth. It was right and necessary that she should look after Naomi. She acknowledged the Lord in all her ways. God acted. He was, by promise, bound to. It is just like my Irish friend, David, who was almost killed in a terrorist bomb explosion. The bomb had injured him in the face and weeks after that deadly hour I was overhauling the universe with him around a blazing fire. What was his reaction to the whole thing? Quietly looking at me he said: "If God can bring order out of the chaos of the cross, He can bring order out of the chaos of my face". Those words are alive in me even now.

She went, and gleaned in the field after the reapers and "her hap was" to light on a part of the field belonging unto Boaz, who was of the kindred of Elimelech. It was a singular field. The system used in the Bethlehem - Judah of those days was different to our idea of farming. We imagine farmers with individual fields owned by the farmer, but this was not the case. There appears to be a common field where all grow their crops, with ownership vested in parts of the one great field. Not hedges but stones separated the various sections.

There is enough in that phrase "Her hap was" to keep me writing until the end of this book. Apparently, by chance, Ruth came to glean corn in a section of the field belonging to a mighty man of wealth called Boaz. The phrase "Her hap was" shows clearly that she did not understand the full significance of what she was doing.

There is the secret. She had acknowledged the Lord, and it was no happening that she walked into Boaz's section, though at the time she thought nothing of it.

Just like Philip. Do you think it was a happening that Philip many centuries later ran and joined himself to a chariot owned by an Ethiopian Government Cabinet Member at the very moment the official was reading a verse about the Lord Jesus that needed explaining? God told Philip to run and if he had not, he would have arrived at the wrong verse. A happening?

> *How much of our life resembles*
> *Time lost in going upstairs;*
> *What days and weeks seem wasted,*
> *But we're climbing unawares.*

The simple fact is that in ten years' time you may look back and find that the most important thing you did this year was to open a door, walk across a street or bump into a friend. Little things have fascinating repercussions. A word here, a word there, can ripple through eternity. Watch the little things. It so happened that a man who cared for young people went into a store in Boston and spoke of the Lord Jesus to a young "shoe-shop" assistant. Nobody knew that that conversation would result in Dwight L. Moody, the young assistant, moving, under God, thousands upon thousands to find the same Lord Jesus. One was C. T. Studd who in turn led thousands in Africa to the Saviour. Another was a lady in Co. Antrim, Ulster, whose son I was preaching with the other night, and he is over sixty years of age!

We could go on! We were standing in the office of Jim Vaus not long ago. His room was filled with huge computers and he was explaining to some doctors about a system he was developing to aid them in administrative work.

As he talked we sat at the back of the room and our minds wandered back to nineteen forty-six when Jim was a notorious criminal with one million dollars to his name accumulated by devious means. His brilliant knowledge of electronics had been used in entirely the wrong direction.

He sat that night listening to a young preacher called Billy Graham as he told of the story of a Saviour's love and how if repenting of sin, a person could find forgiveness and salvation, by accepting the Saviour's death as sufficient in God's eyes to cover all his sins. Jim did just that! The result? As we winged our way home, out of New York, in Jim's little four-seater plane I asked Vaus's pilot-assistant what he thought of his boss. A self-confessed non-Christian, he said: "When Vaus came into this place there were one hundred and forty youth gangs in this area and now there are none!"

Remember this all started when the young Christian whose preaching was used of God to win Jim to saving faith in the nineteen-forties got down on his knees and handed himself over completely to his Master for the preaching of the Gospel. I know, because he told me so himself! Little things. I have come to believe that in life it is the little things that are big and important and the seemingly big things small, empty, boring, and in the end very insignificant. It is like the correspondence between Victor Hugo and his publisher Hurst and Blackell in 1862.

The author was on holiday and anxious to know how his new novel "Les Miserables" was selling. He wrote: "?". The reply was: "!". Little things mean much more than they appear. Watch them as for your very life.

Hard, back-breaking work it was, gleaning. Her very presence there showed that she was in the poverty bracket. Yet, God, ever gracious, had provided for the widows. It was laid down in His law that at harvest time a man must not reap his land to the very border, nor should he pick up what was left after the reapers went through. If he forgot a sheaf and left it in the field he was forbidden to go back for it. That was for the gleaner. I wonder sometimes just what thoughts were Ruth's as she gleaned in the heavy sun. This surely was the path of poverty and brokenness.

Is it any different for those of us who are sick and tired of the standard average life of the Christian world around us?

A life of ease and talk, of looking over the shoulder at each other before we move for God?

Tired of the emptiness of our prayer lives and our own preaching that lacks the sweet, direct, recognisable touch of the Holy Spirit? Those of us, and those would include every man and child who knows and loves the Lord Jesus, who are longing for a mighty revival to be poured out upon our land before the Master returns: and we wait and wait and wait. Wherein lies our weakness?

It lies in our lack of brokenness before God. We must rise from our ease to our knees and tell the Lord that without Him we can do nothing, nothing, NOTHING! It will mean losing the smile of the sophisticated circle; it will mean sacrifice and time alone at His sorely wounded feet. It is not the popular thing . . . it is the only thing.

What do I mean? I mean just this. Let me illustrate: We had been given a direction from God one day to hold an Open Air Service in an Irish country "grazing field" to proclaim the Gospel. It was something which some thought foolish. "We are in a modern society, moon walking and all that . . . modern men do not go to grazing fields to hear the Gospel". Despite the critics we called a day of prayer. There they were - twenty men on their knees for hours. Suddenly as somebody was praying, the tears started pouring down his face. A strange stillness came into the room. Now everybody was sobbing. This was no worked up emotionalism . . . the man who was praying was praying for his wayward daughter who was without the Saviour. Never in all of my life did I sit in a prayer meeting like it. The power from then on was indescribable. When we rose the next day to preach the Gospel in the field to the hundreds gathered, it was no surprise to see them there. Nor was it a surprise in the darkness of the night when an eighteen-year-old came to see us so burdened that she must find Christ as her Saviour before the day ended. She did and she was not the only one.

"Have I been so long with thee,
And yet hast thou not known Me ?
O my Master, I have found Thee
On the roads of Galilee".

"Have I been so long time with thee
On the roads of Galilee,
Yet, My child, thou hast not known Me
Walking on the tossing sea ?"

"O my Master, I have known Thee
On the roads and on the sea".
"Wherefore then hast thou not known Me
Broken in Gethsemane?"

"I would have thee follow, know Me
Thorn-crowned, nailed upon the tree.
Canst thou follow, wilt thou know Me,
All the way to Calvary ?"

The weekend passed and on the Monday night we went to the place of preaching again. At that time it was my privilege to preach with a young local headmaster, Robert Hewitt. Words to describe people are sometimes meaning-less and hard to choose, but suffice is to say that there are few in Ireland like him. Humble, dedicated, down-to-earth with a reserved spirit that adds a touch of gentleness to all that he does. He loves the Lord Jesus dearly. He rose to speak after I was through and suddenly something happened.The tears started to pour down his cheeks. Robert crying!! I had never seen him crying before in my life and I have seen him in some places where anyone would have broken. He was talking about the cross. A power gripped that congregation so much so that my friend, broken under the power of the message, could not go on. He simply sat down and sobbed his heart out. A cultured, college trained, well respected headmaster breaking his heart when describing the sufferings of his Saviour. There, there, there is the secret of power - brokenness! No advertising, no organisation, no oratory, no "plastic" evangelism could do that. Send more and more of it to this island, Lord! Break us! Melt us! Humble us! Be glorified! I could not close the meeting. The whole place was so obviously under the power of the Spirit. I had only heard one man describe such a happening as I was witnessing now. A gentle, humble, Spirit-filled Scottish

Bible teacher, called Albert Leckie whose knowledge of God's Word I have not seen equalled, anywhere. (A second cousin of Edward Heath's, in fact). He told me it once happened to him and the congregation would not go home, but just sat on. It was happening to us. When eventually we did close the meeting in prayer is it any wonder that amongst those converted was the girl for whom her father had wept sore in prayer on the Saturday? I am not advocating emotionalism, but what I am emphasising is brokenness in the presence of our God. He is not some theological nicety. He is alive and real and ready to bless. But, we must have a "Gethsemane experience" as His blessed Son did if we are to have His fellowship. "Not my will - but Thine be done!"

She was only a gleaner amidst alien corn. A lovely girl whose lover had died and living amongst people she did not know. Humble, insignificant and broken. Her back bending to pull at but strands of what others were getting arm loads. It was all that was allowed to her, but God had sent her there. He knew what He was doing; "who never negligently yet fashioned an April violet". She was in the right corner of the field. It may have been a path of brokenness, but it was the path of blessing. In fact, though she was not fully aware of it, it was the path of God.

Across the will of nature,
Leads on the path of God;
Not where the flesh delighteth
The feet of Jesus trod.

O bliss to leave behind us
The fetter of the slave,
To leave ourselves behind us,
The grave clothes and the grave !

We follow in His footsteps:
What if our feet be torn ?
Where He has marked the pathway
All hail the brier and thorn !

Scarce seen, scarce heard, unreckoned,
Despised, defamed, unknown
Or heard but by our saying,
On, children, ever on !

Fields take cultivation,
but it must come slow,
unhurried by the tractor's tread.
Good farmers don't harass the ground
until the ground is ready.
And just as only experts
have the means to teach us hate,
farming is an art form too.

So whether planting love
or lima beans
the careful man goes carefully
down his furrows.

- Rod McKuen

3

Love

He always rubbed his finger up and down the raised book rest on his desk. When emphasising a point he would look over his half-rimmed glasses and catch the head of a small nail on the side of his book rest and squeeze it between his finger and thumb.

I studied his every move because I sat at the desk right at the front of his English class. Norman Watts officially, but to us, privately, he was always Nore. And we loved him.

My pal Cunningham and I used to vie with each other to see who would get the highest marks for "Nore's Essay" set every other weekend. Dear help (it is an Irish expression)

Nore if Cunningham got one more mark than I! We always wanted to know why.

Legends surrounded him in school: most of them were true. He was parachuted into France as a soldier in war-time and walked the length of the land as a Polish farmer! Despite the legends he opened our minds as youngsters to the beauty of words.

I can see him yet with the backdrop of Downpatrick Cathedral and the sun filtering the dust in the room and streaming in the window as Nore would say: "Now watch this word boys. Keats always uses the right word on the right occasion: no other word will do. You cannot find a better description of a glass of wine than 'beaded bubble winking at the brim'. Or on Hamlet, 'when Shakespeare makes ghosts walk- ghosts walk !'" He brought the very best out of you.

The point is that it was Nore who first introduced me to the language of love in poetry. Not old sentiment, but the real thing in words. We will always remember the words of Browning's "Meeting at Night" as Nore taught it. "Listen to the sound coming out in the words boys", he would say...

The grey sea and the long black land;
And the yellow half-moon large and
low;
And the startled little waves that leap
In fiery ringlets from their sleep,
As I gain the cove with pushing prow,
And quench its speed in the slushy sand.

Then a mile of warm sea-scented beach;
Three fields to cross till a farm appears;
A tap at the pane, the quick sharp scratch
And blue spurt of a lighted match,
And a voice less loud, thro' its joy and
fears,
Than the two hearts beating each to each !

It is that last line which is gentle on my mind when I think of Boaz and Ruth. Two hearts beating each to each? It certainly was love at first sight, and "Behold", says the author of Ruth, as if he were adding a fresh touch of vividness to his writing. Behold what? A man has arrived on the scene. No mean man. Wealthy, some even translate it "A mighty man of valour". According to Leon Morris, we get the force of it by thinking of our word "Knight". It seems that added to his money he was a man of great moral worth and his name means "Strength". It is no alien harvest he has come to supervise - it is his own ! "The Lord be with you" he says to the reapers. He knows the Lord too ! What girl would not pray for such a combination in a man; wealthy, full of moral worth, a man of strength (strong, silent type!) and in love with the Lord? Blessed combination.

The eyes of the great man rove the field checking out his workers when suddenly they stop at - Ruth! "Whose damsel is this?" he asks a servant, and the news is not long in coming back. The thing about his servant's answer is that he must have had his eye on Ruth all day because his report was that the young woman (damsel) was the one that came back with Naomi and that she had "continued even from the morning until now, that she tarried a little in the house". That simply means that he had even noticed the break she had taken in the house, probably adjacent to the field being reaped. She was being watched.

Now comes the blessing. Somebody had heard of her plight, though she did not know it. Walking quietly up to her Boaz lays his blessing upon her young life. He had heard of her faithfulness. He knew of the separation from her father, mother and the land of her nativity. He knew that she had come unto a people "which thou knewest not". He knew it and he told her so.

Best of all, he recognised that the Lord God of Israel was the One "under whose wings thou art come to trust".He tells her to go to no other field. If thirsty, she is to drink of the water his young men have drawn and warned the same young men not to touch her. Why that warning? The single reason is that the enthusiasm of gleaners some-times carried them beyond their allotted area; they came too close to the reapers, annoyed them and they were sometimes forced to drive them back. Ruth was not to be touched. She was to be left alone. And more, much more. At meal-time she sat by the reapers, dipped her bread in vinegar and Boaz handed her parched corn, "and she did eat, and was sufficed". Parched corn? As W. M. Thompson points out in his book "The Land of the Book"; "A quantity of the best ears, not too ripe are plucked with the stalks attached. These are tied into small parcels, a blazing fire is kindled with dry grass and thorn bushes, and the corn heads are held in it until the chaff is mostly burned off. The grain is thus sufficiently roasted to be eaten, and it is a favourite article all over the country". She goes back to her work and Boaz tells his young men to "let fall some of the handfuls of purpose for her", as an extra thrown in.

When writing this last paragraph I received a telephone call from a very dedicated Christian woman known to all and sundry as Peggy. She is a very wonderful mother of seven children and is a fund of knowledge on everything from a needle to how to handle preachers ! When I am on a writing spree she rings me up to see how things are going and to pass on her thought for the day. Today's was particularly apt. "Did you ever think about that verse which says 'My God shall supply all your need according to his riches in glory by Christ Jesus'?" she asked me over a telephone line that connected one hundred miles of Ireland that lay between us. I said I had. "Did you notice it says, supply all your NEED. That simply means you don't get the supply until you have the need!" What a very obvious but profound thought. As each need arises,

He supplies it. You didn't get that prayer answered because the Lord did not feel that today was the time you needed it answered. He never keeps anything in His plan for your life that you need now. God's supply and demand system is different to ours. The prodigal son grabs all and runs, but when the world's supply proves that there is a hole in the bucket and he discovers he needs his father's love and care, behold, there it is!

God is like that. The whole world was lost in the darkness of sin. Mankind was separated from Him; there was no mediator. Then at the very time when we were without strength, God acted. He saw our need. We were strangers from the Commonwealth of Israel and the Covenants of Promise. Like Ruth we were picking up just what we could find and not making much of it.

We were thirsting and we knew that we could not live by bread alone. Lonely, searching, and heading for trouble. God's love spotted us. He sent that Precious Baby to Bethlehem. He led Him through childhood to manhood. His will was to do His Father's will and that led to the depths of Gethsemane, the journey to the judgment hall and the darkness of Calvary. When we were without strength, Christ died for us ! When we were Godless, Christ died for the ungodly! God loved the world -good. Christ loved the Church -better. But the Son of God who loved ME and gave Himself for me - absolutely supreme ! No person was ever born again of the Spirit of God without first learning their need of Him! When, by faith, we discover that our need is supplied.

Our sins were not only forgiven, but this heavenly Boaz did much more ! He quenched our thirst. I love F. B. Meyer's commentary on John 4 and the woman at the well. He says:

"'Whosoever drinketh of this water, shall thirst again' is a legend that might be engraved on Jacob's well: and equally in every theatre, and other place of worldly amusement or sin, the votaries of which get sips, not draughts; but this would satisfy. In the failure of human love, in the absence of blessed friendships and companionships, in the subsidence of every Cherith brook, those who received what He longed to bestow should never thirst".

May we in turn,

As from far untrodden snow
Of Lebanon the streams run free,
Dear Lord, command our streams to flow,
That thirsty men may drink of Thee.

Then of course He gave us bread - fed us until we wanted no more. Like Ruth, "we were sufficed". No wonder we fall at His feet, and like Ruth say "Why have I found grace in thine eyes, that thou shouldst take knowledge of me, seeing I am a stranger?" Why did the Lord Jesus pick me out? Why you? Why, when millions in this modern age rush on to eternity with no thought of spiritual things, did the Lord Jesus by His Spirit find me in the field ("the field is the world", Mark 4) and give me food, drink, and set me in His banqueting house and His banner over me was - Love?

Then, as if that were not enough, He drops handfuls of purpose for me along the way. Why? My dear reader, if I could answer that question I would be God. "I know not why, I only cry, Oh, how He loves me!"

I may be wrong, but I strongly suspect that Boaz was deeply in love from the very first glance. Is there anything wrong with that?

Though cities bow to art, and I am its own true lover,
It is not art, but heart, which wins the wide world over.

Dr. Boreham once wrote of an eminent pianist whose recitals crowded the most spacious auditoriums in Europe with ecstatic audiences. Yet there was just one thing lacking in his life. This brilliant pianist was a lonely, taciturn man and a certain coldness and aloofness would steal into his playing from time to time. At that time there also lived another much older pianist whose name was a household word in musical circles the wide world over. One day this person laid their hand upon the shoulder of the brilliant younger performer and said: "Will you let me tell you, my boy, that your playing lacks one thing. So far you have missed the greatest thing in the world. And, unless you fall in love, there will always be a certain cold perfection about your music. Unless you come to love another human being passionately and unselfishly, you will never touch human hearts as deeply as you might".

As in the natural and physical, so in the spiritual. Methinks I detect in my Christian service a very similar "coldness and aloofness". Mechanical, technical, theological - but dry. Often it is because my love for my Lord has grown very cold. As someone once said "we take it for granted that we preach Christ because we love Christ"; but *is the assumption always safe?* It was many centuries ago that one of the greatest christians who ever lived wrote from a prison cell:

"If I had the gift of being able to speak in other languages without learning them, and could speak in every language there is in all of heaven and earth, but didn't love others, I would only be making noise. If I had the gift of prophecy and knew all about what is going to happen in the future, knew everything about everything, but didn't love others, what good would it do? Even if I had the gift of faith so that I could speak to a mountain and make it move, I would still be worth nothing at all without love. If I gave everything I have to poor people, and if I were burned alive for preaching the Gospel but didn't love others, it would be of no value whatever".

"Love is very patient and kind, never jealous or envious, never boastful or proud, never haughty or selfish or rude. Love does not demand its own way. It is not irritable or touchy. It does not hold grudges and will hardly even notice when others do it wrong. It is never glad about injustice, but rejoices whenever truth wins out. If you love someone you will be loyal to him no matter what the cost. You will always believe in him, always expect the best of him, and always stand your ground in defending him".

"All the special gifts and powers from God will some day come to an end, but love goes on for ever".

Mere sentiment - no sir!

I sometimes remind myself of the story Catherine Marshall tells about the dream she had about her husband Peter. She was discussing with her husband the biography of his life that she was occupied in writing when he laid down a condition. What was the condition? "Tell the world, Catherine, that a man can love the Lord and not be a cissy!" I like it.

It's the heart where the summer is moulded
And woven the magical blue,
And always a glory is folded
That waits but a welcome from you.
The world is the world that you make it,
A dungeon, a desert, a bower;
The sunshine is falling and cuckoos are
calling
If only the heart is in flower.

When the Rose of Sharon blooms there - all is well!

4

At His Feet

I have discovered a strange thing. Sometimes whenever feet and the Lord Jesus are mentioned in the New Testament, there is criticism. Mary sat at His feet and was scolded by Martha. Another Mary poured ointment on His feet and was scolded by the Pharisees. Jesus went to wash the disciples' feet and was scolded by Peter.

Let us, for a second, look at this phenomenon.

My mother was not a philosopher or a great theologian in terms of the great women in the history of the Church. Her name will not be found in the annals of some great library, but as far as I and those who were privileged to be near to her were concerned, the spiritual things she taught us will be forever in our hearts. Her name was written in Heaven when one day as a girl she accepted the Lord Jesus as her Saviour and that's what REALLY mattered to her. One day she came running into my room, Bible in hand. "Look at this", she exclaimed. Look at what? "The story of Mary and Martha".

For twenty minutes she sat down and poured out some gleanings she had gained from her quiet reading of the story. My mum had little time for commentaries and read little but pure scripture. The point she emphasised to me that day was what Jesus said of Mary, who sat at His feet. He said that she had "chosen that better part, which shall not be taken away from her"! Looking at me with determination mother declared: "Shall not be taken away in time or eternity! To sit at Jesus feet is an eternal blessing! What you gain there you simply cannot lose. It goes on with you forever. It will NEVER be taken away from you, son!"

As I sit here writing today I think of my mother, lying, dying of cancer. After a life of unending faithfulness to her Lord, her evangelist husband, and to us as boys, she has to face - this! Anybody who has ever lived in a house with a cancer patient will know what I am talking about. Deadly enemy!

About a week before she died I remember coming in from school teaching, and after throwing my books down I gently knocked on her door. Standing at the bottom of her bed, I faced her square.

"Now mother, honestly tell me. Are you afraid to die? You may think it a strange question, but at this stage of your life, is the Lord Jesus as real to you as when you were without pain? I have got to know".

She pointed to the lovely text on the wall above her which two dedicated Christian nurses had given her:

"Thou shalt keep him in *perfect peace* whose mind is stayed upon thee". "That is what I have got", she said.

Now tell me, where did my mother originally get that peace? She got it one day by faith, as a ten-year-old girl kneeling at the sore wounded feet of a living Christ. She used to tell me over and over again that she had no great vision, no text, no preacher near her, but in trusting Him she got peace. The burden went. As we laid her in the cemetery, I could not forget her words to me:

"Shall not be taken away! . . . in time or eternity. To sit at Jesus feet is an eternal blessing! What you gain there you simply cannot lose. It goes on with you forever. It will NEVER be taken away from you, son! " I can see her in glory enjoying it now.

In Luke seven we read of a nameless woman who had not a reputation that was fragrant. "A woman in the city which was a sinner", says Luke. What caused her to stand behind the Son of God, weeping, would interest me greatly. Did she see that Simon, the Pharisee, had not even had the courtesy to offer water for His hot and tired feet? Did her heart not move within her as she saw the callousness of the men who cared so much for the letter of the law and were very careless about the Master of it? I wish I had words to grip the meaning of the phrase, "She stood at His feet weeping", yet she did not stand long because soon she was on her knees and was wiping those feet with the hairs of her head, kissing them and anointing them with oil. He is, you see, the sinners' Saviour. The religious nation of Israel pierced His feet with nails, but a sinful woman kissed them. He came not to call the righteous but sinners to repentance. Simon thought only of the outward, for he reckoned a woman of her calibre could only be capable of one thing. He was wrong - what she was doing would never be taken away from her, for the same principle applies to her as applied to the other Mary. How? Did not Jesus say, "Wheresoever the gospel shall be preached in the whole world, there shall also this, that this woman hath done, be told for a *memorial* to her". It shall not be taken away from her. You see, getting down at Jesus feet involves the low place. He becomes the focus of all that we do, our directions come from Him. When you abandon yourself to that position, look out, for the devil will be on your track. He was on Mary's, but she cared not. There is the place of power. To sit and learn of Him, to saturate your mind and heart with his humility and fragrance. There is true success.

Ruth got there. Quietly, stealthily, she walked down to the threshing-floor. The Bible says she went down and I would take that simply to mean that Bethlehem was ridged and normally although one would go up to a threshing-floor, she had to go down to the building in order to climb. It was night and no one saw her. She had bathed (lit. meaning of 'wash' in the text), anointed herself and went down to where Boaz lay sleeping on the threshing-floor. Not a sound was heard as she quietly uncovered his feet of the cloak that covered them, and lay down, at the end of "the heap of corn". Not a stir. She lay there gently, quietly, waiting.

Now I fully realise that this is a most difficult point. It is amazing how expositors of the Bible always fight shy of questions on the chapter. I have asked quite a few, and they just pass this action off as "custom", and will not be drawn any further. Some custom! It certainly was not attested other than here. Was she not going too far? Was she pushing this man's gentleness?

No, I do not believe it. It will take a little explanation. Naomi's plans in sending Ruth to the threshing-floor certainly had its dangers, but she obviously trusted her. As we shall see, she had a right to be there. Yet interwoven into this story is the great scriptural thread of God's brinkmanship. Let me explain.

In Israel when a man died it was decreed that the brother of the deceased was to marry the widow. If he refused then the woman could publicly humiliate him. Naomi probably knew that there was another kinsman other than Boaz, but calculated that he would not redeem Ruth so she reckoned on introducing Ruth to Boaz first. Boaz was, of course, directly related to Naomi and was in line to redeem Ruth's seed. So that young woman lying at the feet of Boaz was showing him by her action that she was willing to be redeemed. Whither her action was right or wrong, she was staking her claim. She wanted the redemption which he could offer, and she lay at his feet and was waiting to see what he would do. She took the lowest place.

We have come across the word "Behold" in this story before, and here it is again. The first time was when his eyes fell on Ruth, the second was "and it came to pass at midnight, that the man was afraid, and turned himself, and, behold, a woman lay at his feet". Behold indeed! When Ruth gives her identity and reminds him that he is a "near kinsman", it soon becomes obvious that a great moment had arrived. Let us hold it there a moment.

God had promised in the very beginning, after sin entered our universe, to send His Son into the world. Did you ever stop to think how it often seemed as though He was going to break His promise? When the huge floods burst on the earth and a boat held eight people out of the whole of earth's population it did not look as though the coming Messiah was going to come from that line. Yet, they were preserved. Talk about brinkmanship! When God promised Abram that through his seed all the nations of the earth would be blessed it certainly did not look like it when he was asked to raise his knife and slay Isaac. Yet, there was a ram caught in the thicket. Talk about brinkmanship! Six feet of air between a knife and death.

Then there were Israel's escapes. The number of times when it was only a lonely man on Sinai called Moses that pleaded with God to preserve them, would amaze you. Count them sometime. But then, one with God is a majority. The line was preserved yet again.

To think of Ruth quietly claiming her right to be redeemed on a threshing-floor in Bethlehem as, though she did not know it, actually preserving the line of the Messiah, is a tremendous moment in this great story.

Take Hezekiah when God told him to set his house in order for he was to die and not live. He turned his head to the wall and wept, pleading with God to preserve him. He was given fifteen extra years and in that time a son was born to him, who carried on that Royal line. Why does God sometimes move to the very brink?

It is God's nature to show that the wisdom of men is but foolishness with Him. Man delights in showing his wisdom, but God delights in hiding things from the wise and prudent and revealing them unto babes. Like a quiet, insignificant, peasant girl called Mary, for instance, locked out of an inn, though expecting a little one. Given no place in the eyes of men, just one in a crowd, yet given by God the greatest privilege ever given to womanhood: to give birth to the Prince of Peace. God does not act in some great fanfare - He uses humble, obedient people, one here, one there, because He

"Hath chosen the foolish things of the world
To confound the wise,
. . . the weak things of the world,

To confound the mighty.

... base things of the world ... which are despised,

Things which are not to bring to nought things that are,

That no flesh should glory in His presence".

Greatest of all, is Calvary; so despised by the world Darkness, seeming defeat, weak in the eyes of men. The world thought it was the end of the road, but little did they realise that it was the greatest victory ever won. No wonder Paul (I like sometimes to call him Mr. Greatheart!) said: "For though He was crucified through weakness, yet He liveth by the power of God!" Tell me, reader, have you been to Calvary? Have you repented of your sin and put your trust in the precious blood shed there for your sin. It is the blood of Jesus Christ, His Son, that cleanseth us from all sin. It seems weak in human terms, but, as Paul adds, "We also are weak WITH (margin) Him, but we shall live with Him by the power of God towards you". In Christ we have everything, without Him, nothing.

At His feet! Do you despise that place? Maybe a Christian reader is feeling despised because of the seemingly insignificant role you have been given by the Lord. Could I quote to you a beautiful piece of writing which means a lot to me? I don't know where I found it, I don't know who wrote it, but here it is:

"I was tired and sat down under the shadow of the great pines in a Swedish forest, glad to find such a cool retreat from the broiling sun. I had not been there long before I noticed a fragrant odour and wondered what it could be and where it came from.

"No Marechal Niel rose grew on that barren soil, nor could the sun penetrate the shades of the forest to extract its perfume even if it had; I looked round, and found by my side a tiny flower about half the size of an ordinary daisy, nearly hidden from view by the moss. It was the little 'Linea blomma'.

"Oh, how fragrant it smelt! Again and again I held it near my face, enjoying the perfume, and then I looked up and thanked God for that tiny flower so insignificant, growing in a wild, almost untrodden forest, yet bringing cheer and refreshment to me.

"I thought, why is it so obscure, when it is a flower with such fragrance, and surely worthy of a place in the most stately grounds? I learned a lesson by it, and it spoke powerfully to my heart.

"I thought, if I cannot be a pine in God's forest, I may be a tiny flower to send forth the fragrance of Jesus in this world of sadness".

There is a tendency in our hearts to desire to be or to do something great. We may not be content, like the tiny linea flower, to send forth fragrance in obscurity.

I have often met the Lord's people despondent over the apparent uselessness of their lives. They cannot point to some great feat accomplished for the Lord. It has never been theirs to figure prominently in His service, nor have they the remembrance of having done anything worthy of the record.

It is written, "Seekest thou great things for thyself? seek them not" (Jer. 45:5). Beloved fellow believers, let me tell you it is possible for you to be fragrant in this world. Keep close to Christ, walk in happy communion with Him; let your heart drink in His love and you will be fragrant to Him.

Could you conceive anything greater than that? No eye may see you but His, no ear hear you but His, no heart appreciate your act or thought but His; yet how precious, I can be fragrant to the Lord Jesus ! Nothing surely is so delightful to Him as to have you and me walking with Himself. If this is so, we shall also surely come in contact with some weary soul who needs refreshment. We can speak of Jesus, and in such a way that there will be a Christ-likeness about us. Let us give up the disappointing business of self-occupation. As long as we are occupied with self, we are not occupied with Christ. True greatness is the measure in which the excellence of Christ flows forth from us.

"His name is as ointment poured forth". He was not great as men count greatness. He chose no place of prominence. When by force they would make Him king, He retired; when His brethren pressed Him to go up to the feast to do some great miracle and make Himself prominent, He answered, "My time is not yet come".

To do His Father's will was His one commanding business. Oh ! that "Plant of renown", that "Branch of David's stem", that

"Root out of a dry ground", who could say: "All my springs are in thee".

What fragrance came forth from Him! Those who were far from God could smell the holy perfume, and say: "Never man spake like this man". The heartless Pilate had to say, "I find no fault in this man". The centurion at the cross had to confess, "Certainly this was a righteous man". Others could but marvel at "the gracious words that proceeded out of his mouth".

None could come into His presence without smelling the fragrant odours of love, compassion and tenderness. The wickedness of the human heart, which He met on every hand, only disclosed His preciousness more and more. Let us then not be despondent over what we are and what we are not. Let our attention be more than ever directed to Him, so that as He fills our vision everything else may vanish. As His sweetness fills the soul, so will His fragrance flow forth from us as the outcome of communion with Him.

May the Lord, then, so attach your hearts to Himself that, like the little Linea flower, sending forth its odour in the untrodden forest, we may send forth by His Spirit and for

His own pleasure something of His fragrance, in this world where He is not, and so become a reflection of the only perfect and fragrant One, Jesus!

God of the heights, austere, inspiring,
Thy word hath come to me,
O let no selfish aims conspiring
Distract my soul from Thee.
Loosen me from things of time,
Strengthen me for steadfast climb.

The temporal would bind my spirit;
Father, be Thou my stay.
Show me what flesh cannot inherit
Stored for another day.
Be transparent, things of time.
Looking through you, I would climb.

Now by Thy grace my spirit chooseth,
Treasure that shall abide.
The great unseen, I know, endureth,
My footsteps shall not slide.
Not for me the things of time,
God of the mountain, I will climb.

5

A Man's Reaction

Have you ever seen a round peg trying to get in a square hole? It happens every day. The speaker rises to speak with the words, "Now I'm no speaker . . . but". Twenty minutes later (or even less) it is obvious to everybody that he is just exactly what he said he was - no speaker. Much better to be thought a fool than to open your mouth and remove all doubt ! Great cooks being waiters when they should be in the kitchen, young men who love and were brought up to love farming and wide open spaces spending their days in a stuffy city office because they think that is the way to sophistication. Thousands of people in the wrong jobs!

Yet to see a man doing his job who really knows how to do it is a beautiful thing to watch. The craftsman at the potter's wheel; the natural teacher bending over a pupil with a problem; the dedicated, happy, doctor tickling his little child patient and giving it a reassuring smile and goading it back to health; the strong arm of the gifted, spiritual pastor as he gently leads a wayward christian back onto a better path; the gifted evangelist as he burns the flame of his message before the thoughtless men of the world in language they understand; the gifted, gentle, Bible teacher as he unravels the gems of God's word and feeds the flock instead of flogging them.

We all know gift when we see it. Gift does not need to trumpet to draw attention to its qualities. It is as clear as day. Gift always makes way for itself. You have a gift given you of God - use it! Don't, for any sake, try to be somebody else.

Whatever you are- be that,
Whatever you say - be true,
Straightforwardly act- be honest, in fact
Be nobody else but you.

Boaz, to me at least, was a natural. I imagine him to be the kind of person you could go to when in trouble. Gentle, warm, sensitive. Always beware of the man who is hard in spirit - he is usually hiding something. I can see another man reacting in the situation Boaz found himself in.

A young woman, beautiful Ruth, lay at his feet, claiming marriage. It was night. No one had seen her come. They were alone. Yet, here was no silly old fool. Here was no village lout. Here was a gentleman. Boaz, who had at the very roots of his manly nature the two rare qualities of twentieth century men, dignity and restraint.

Gently he talks to Ruth in the quietness and stillness, his accent calming her fears. Spiritual and manly.

"Blessed be thou of the Lord, my daughter; for thou hast shewed more kindness in the latter end than at the beginning . . . I will do all that thou requirest for all the city of my people know that thou art a virtuous woman".

It was her sense of the RIGHT that impressed him. She had not followed after other men, whether rich or poor. Boaz was in line to redeem her, and to Boaz she came.

By his very definition of Ruth as 'a virtuous woman' he certainly shows that as far as he was concerned there was no impropriety in what Ruth had done. Before she leaves, Boaz asks her to hold her cloak out and into it he measures eighty pounds of barley!

His gift was love and care: he showed it perfectly. What if he had refused? What if he had turned her away? There was no sign of it. He was not ashamed of her.

It is not, of course, within my powers to adequately describe the Lord Jesus who was not ashamed of me when I came to Him for redemption. Many pens have tried and failed. What if He had not fulfilled His promise ? What if He let me lie there? Yet He did not. He not only filled my cloak with plenty but He gave His precious blood to redeem me. Did you ever try to think of just how precious that blood was?

Robert McLuckie is a most lovable Scotsman; to the core, in fact. He even claims that Scotland is God's very own country! One day he took me for a walk around Edinburgh Castle and glowed as he described the historical background of Edinburgh Castle and tradition of his land as symbolised in that great citadel. By and by he took me into the throne room, and there in a casket lay the crown jewels of Scotland. The central crown really drew my attention and turning to the assistant who stood by with his long coat and many buttons I queried, 'How much is it worth?'

I was amazed at his reaction. He was flaming angry. "How much is it worth?" he reiterated. "Yes, thirty million, forty million. Surely there must be some price on it?" "Young man" he said emphatically, "three thousand men died in one day to put that crown on the head of Robert the Bruce. If you want to put a price upon human blood you are welcome to try. The crown is priceless!" As he defused, and Robert and I beat a hasty retreat, my friend smiled at me when we were at a safe distance and said, "You've got a sermon there, lad ! " He was right. "If you want to put a price upon human blood you are welcome to try". Surely if we cannot attempt to put a price upon the blood of Scotsmen who died in battle, how, just how, can we put a price on that precious blood that stained the hill of Calvary ? Divine life, become human life that we might have everlasting life. The answer is simple - it is priceless, and Peter put it this way: "For we are not redeemed with corruptible things such as silver and gold, but with the precious blood of Christ as of a lamb without blemish and without spot". That was the price of redemption for us: nothing less would satisfy God, and it does. Doesn't it satisfy you?

It is there that the rest of the true christian comes. He made peace through the blood of His cross. Rest is one of the key words in the book of Ruth. Naomi sent Ruth to Boaz with the question "Shall I not seek rest for thee, that it may be well with thee?" She sent her to the right man. Tell me, where do you go for rest? Do you go where so many young folk go in this generation? For an hour I talked to a fellow the other night who longed for rest and the ultimate. He was given some drugs at a beach party on one of our nearby beaches and he found his rest all right - for about an hour. He soon woke up with a craving for more and more and . . . Months later, as a broken, brain stormed lad he admitted to me that it could not satisfy. Try them all. Drink. Permissiveness. Entertainment. They all fail - but the Lord Jesus, never! He does what drugs or anything else can never do. Like another drug-taker I came into contact with recently. In the middle of the night he wandered into our room where we were working and pointed a line out of a book to us. It was one of Arthur Blessitt's books where Arthur had been quoting from the Bible. What did it say? This: "New creature in Christ Jesus . . ."

"I want that", he said. He was looking in the right direction.

Ruth, carrying her burden, now returns home. Eagerness describes her conversation as she pours out all that has happened to her mother-in-law, yet, I suspect Ruth suffered from a very common modern complaint - nerves! Is it too good to be true? The questions arise in her heart. Is he really going to redeem me? The reason I pose these questions is simply because her mother-in-law began to gently upbraid her. "Sit still, my daughter, until thou know how the matter will fall . . ." Sit still, relax!

Doubt is one of the greatest enemies of the christian. I have yet to meet a man who has not had an attack of doubt at some stage. In the problems of human life there come those moments when people begin to doubt, especially when things go wrong. They put their trust in the Lord Jesus but, like Peter, when by the various circumstances of life their eyes go from Him, they begin to sink. The doubting castle of Bunyan's day is just as solid today. Intellectual doubts. Young people questioning everything. Their teachers teaching them to doubt sometimes. Why, I lunched with a Bavarian doctor this very day who told me that the man in his "church" pulpit did not believe in eternal life! It was pretty obvious to me that he knew nothing about it. Europe may seem to breed doubters, but amidst it all there are those whose faith is resting in the Rock of Ages. They believe that theirs is not an unreasonable faith but that it is beyond reason. What word could be given to the true believers who are in Doubting Castle? Just this! Naomi has a word for Ruth.

"Sit still . . . for the man will not be in rest until he has finished the thing this day". If Boaz said he would do it, then he would do it. If God says He will save you if you trust His Son, then He will do just that. If God says "Delight thyself also in the Lord and he shall give thee the desires of thine heart", He will not rest until it is done. While we stumble and stray here, the Lord never rests working for us. While Ruth worried, Boaz was in the city busy knocking down the problems, one by one!

Our God neither slumbers nor sleeps. Away, young person with your doubting - He shall not rest until He has finished the thing for you, this day! Did Karl Marx ever reach down and give you peace? Have existentialists like Jean Paul Satre ever given you one minute's rest of mind and heart? You can philosophise, argue, call it relativity, conditioning or anything else you like to call it, but one thing I know - once I was restless, purposeless, empty and lost, now I have, the Lord Jesus. Like you, maybe, I too have sat listening to hundreds of lectures given by the greatest of minds, but they never, ever, gave me what I got through the victory of Calvary - a Holy Spirit to guide me, a salvation to save me, and a Christ to redeem me. I do not understand all this; do not begin to understand it; never expect to understand it. Yet I realise that it meets the deepest needs of my heart.

For a thousand reasons I feel that I am but a little child, and need a Father; I am a sinful man and I desperately need a Saviour; I am troubled and heartbroken, and I need the Spirit, the Comforter. If He shall not rest, day or night, working at God's right hand on our behalf, then what cause have we to fear? Sit still!

One final thing. There is another question which christian young people in particular are always asking - I want this or that desperately and the Lord does not answer me. If He shall not rest concerning me, what's holding Him up on the answer? I was in a newspaper editor's office the other day and someone had stuck on the very desk in front of me this verse that we are talking about. Girls in particular seem to hold on to the promise, but think the Lord is slow on answering. To you I can only quote a favourite poem. To Ruth the Lord said "yes" on this particular issue; to you -

> *Just a lovely little child,*
> *Three years old,*
> *And a mother with a heart*
> *All of gold,*
> *Often did that mother say*
> *Jesus hears us when we pray,*
> *For He's never far away,*
> *And He always answers.*

Now that tiny little child
Had brown eyes,
And she wanted blue instead,
Like blue skies,
For her mother's eyes were blue,
Like forget-me-nots. She knew
All her mother said was true,
Jesus always answered.

So she prayed for two blue eyes,
Said 'Goodnight',
Went to sleep in deep content,
And delight.
Woke up early, climbed a chair .
By a mirror. Where, O where
Could the blue eyes be? not there;
Jesus hadn't answered.

Hadn't answered her at all;
Never more
Could she pray; her eyes were brown
As before.
Did a little soft wind blow?
Came a whisper soft and low,
Jesus answered. He said 'No';
Isn't No an answer?

6

'Till Happiness Steps Up To Greet Me'

"If we saw the whole, we should see that the Father is doing little else in the world but training His vines"
- Robert Murray McCheyne

Do you believe that everything that happens to you is in a plan? Everything? The mistakes along with the success? The tears that blind along with the pounding heart? The days when you could rip your telephone out of the wall and the days when you could ring the whole world. The times when those children of yours drive you into despair and the days you could cuddle the life out of them. The cycle of life: marriage - birth - death. Is every second, minute, hour, day, month, year, decade of your life part of a plan outside of yourself and directed by the God of Eternity?

For the christian, the answer is yes, if the rules we talked about in chapter two are obeyed. If we are not guided by the Lord and know that ALL things work together for good to them that love Him, the whole point of following Him would be pretty hopeless. But why. before God can bring Ruth to the place of security, rest and happiness did she have to go through so much? This chapter deals with the success of God's great plan, for all God's plans are successful, but why must we have to walk through fields of alien corn first?

Ellice Hopkins once put it this way:

"Do you know the lovely fact about the opal? That, in the first place, it is made only of a desert dust, sand, silica, and owes its beauty and preciousness to a defect. It is a stone with a broken heart. It is full of minute fissures which admit air, and the air reflects the light. Hence its lovely hues, and that sweet lamp of fire that ever burns at its heart, for the breath of the Lord God is in it.

"You are only conscious of the cracks and desert dust, but so He makes His precious opal. We must be broken in ourselves before we can give back the lovely hues of His light, and the lamp in the temple can burn in us and never go out".

We have dealt with this subject of brokenness before in this book, but before we tell of Ruth in her bliss let us remember the long, difficult path that led up to it. It is you see, my friend Ernie Shanks who is continually reminding me of it. Ernie has, at this time of writing, no kidneys. He had them both removed recently and awaits a transplant. I went to see him to try and bring him some comfort the other day. The intensive care unit was most foreboding; all who entered must be clothed from head to toe with protecting garments to shield Ernie from germs.

Slipping a small Bible into my garment I went in and sat beside his bed. Yet, a strange thing occurred. I did not do the talking: he did. Inspiration did not come from me - it came from him. The radiant smile was not on my face - it was on his.

When, eventually, he left hospital and I got him to take part in some evangelistic meetings, it was Ernie who had the power. I took an unconverted socialite to one of those meetings and he was so impressed he rang up the hospital when he got home from the meeting and offered them his kidney! When Ernie rises to speak, people sit up and listen. I have seen him lead a great congregation in singing and hardly a dry eye in the place. Why such power? Why is Ernie "on fire" for the Lord Jesus? Simply because, like the opal, he owes the beauty and fragrance of his life to a defect that he left in the hands of His Master and is content to leave it there. Some of us with no physical defects are miserable. Lord, set us on fire, but help us to be content to go through alien corn first, whatever it costs - like Ernie!

There were ten elders at the gate of the city that day surrounded by a speculative crowd, for the whole world loves a lover. It must have been a heart-throbbing scene for Ruth as her redeemer stands looking at the man next in line to redeem her. He is called in Biblical terms, the kinsman. He is unmarried and, I judge, significantly. Boaz points out to him that Naomi has a piece of land to sell which he has a right to buy. Would he redeem it? He was willing.

Now Boaz comes to the crux of the matter. Ruth, the Moabitess as well as Naomi, is concerned with this field. If the kinsman is to redeem the field then this involves marrying

Ruth, the widow of a childless kinsman in order to have a child to carry on the inheritance. In other words if he is to buy the field then he must in addition provide for Ruth. The problem was there before him. It is obvious that the kinsman was certainly ready to buy the field without marrying Ruth, and he may well have been even ready to marry Ruth without buying the field. What he could not face was doing the two things. It would mar his inheritance. "I cannot redeem it", he says. I leave you to conjecture why. He certainly was not willing to redeem all that she was and had.

Not so Boaz. I can see the kinsman, according to ancient custom, drawing off his shoe, and handing it to Boaz to indicate the withdrawal of his claim to redeem and inviting Boaz to take it up ! What a moment in our story as the crowd gather at the gate of the city to watch this amazing transaction - for the gate of a city in Judah tended to become the very centre of city life. The words ring out clear and plain as the redeemer makes his great speech:

"Ye are witnesses this day, that I have bought all that was Elimelech's, and all that was Chilion's and Mahlon's, of the hand of Naomi. Moreover Ruth the Moabitess, the wife of Mahlon, have I purchased to be my wife, to raise up the name of the dead upon his inheritance, that the name of the dead be not cut off from among his brethren, and from the gate of his place: ye are witnesses this day".

The emphasis I would draw here would lie on that phrase - "I have bought *all* that was Elimelech's, and all that was Chilion's and Mahlon's, of the hand of Naomi ... Moreover Ruth". Let us not forget that this great story of love was written for our learning. This book fits perfectly into the great pattern of God's divine revelation to man. Here in this very speech is the doctrine of man. Elimelech means "My God is King". In that Hebrew name we have God's purpose for man. We're born to let God have supremacy in all things. Elimelech married Naomi which means "Pleasure". Man, in the garden did that very thing by obeying his own desires rather than God's, and it very quickly turned to Mara - bitterness. These two sons "Sickness" and "Pining away" were the result. Yet man was stiffnecked because he went on stubbornly like Orpah - "Stiffnecked". Then came Ruth - "Beautiful", who obeyed God and through Boaz, the man of strength, we hear him redeeming all that was Elimelech's, Mahlon's, Chilion's, Ruth's and Naomi's. What a circle! -but it is not complete yet: watch.

Boaz marries Ruth and slowly the circle takes its last curve. Ruth, who is hailed as better than seven sons (the perfect family), bears a son whose name is Obed. The name is more than significant. What does it mean? Some render it servant; others render it worship, but both give the idea of humility and obedience. What, you ask me, do you mean by the fact that the circle is not complete? I mean just this. This amazing love story ends with a genealogy. Now, that in modern writing is a most unromantic way to end any story. Yet, if you look closely enough you will see that it could not be more romantic. For Boaz begat Obed, and Obed begat Jesse, and Jesse begat David. What is so amazing about that? David was - the King! What a circle from the first tragedy of Elimelech, 'My God is King' in famine and death to Obed, the servant to David - the King! As for God, His way is perfect, for in that very town centuries later David's greater Son came to redeem not only all that was Elimelech's, Mahlon's, Chilion's, Naomi's and Ruth, but to you and me and all men, women, boys and girls who will put their trust in Him.

Did we not say when we first set off on our stroll amidst alien corn that we would see that something beautiful always comes out of the tragic, if God is trusted. It is no different today. As you and I say goodbye, let me say just one final word.

Whether it be the unending tragedy of this island on which I live, the cancer that surrounds us, poverty, death, no matter what, God is not dead. He is always working out His purpose in Christ. He is a happy young person who rests at the Saviour's feet. Whom He loves, He chastens; the end product is the thing that matters. Ruth certainly was wise to say, "Thy God shall be my God". She may have seemed to her friends peculiar, but better a thousand times effective peculiarly than uneffective ordinariness. Her complete subordination to a single aim was absolute. No person who goes for that aim with single-heartedness can fail, God promises, repeat, promises, that "them that honour Me, I will honour".

Ruth's marriage to Boaz was God's doing. No more gleaning for Ruth - she now had the hand of the man who owned the whole field. It is my prayer that you, if you know not Christ, will no longer wander the world trying to glean a little here and there - but rather that you will put your hand in the hand of the One who owns it all. Again, if you do know Him, go and enjoy all the privileges that are yours - go to His storehouse, of which you are a joint heir in Christ, and see if He will not open the windows of heaven, and pour you out a blessing, that there shall not be room enough to receive it. It involves your all, but it ends far from gleaning alien corn. The end-it will explain. It ends in having - Him.

Will not the end explain
The crossed endeavour, earnest purpose
foiled.
The strange bewilderment of good work
spoiled,
The clinging weariness, the inward strain,
Will not the end explain?

Meanwhile He comforteth
Them that are losing patience. 'Tis His
way:
But none can write the words they hear
Him say
For men to read; only they know He saith
Sweet words, and comforteth.

Not that He doth explain
The mystery that baffleth; but a sense
Husheth the quiet heart, that far, far hence
Lieth a field set thick with golden grain
Wetted in seedling days by many a rain:
The end - it will explain.

The EDGE Of DESPAIR

Derick Bingham Looks At Twelve Psalms That Draw You Back

The Psalms are the universal language of the human soul. millions of people from every walk of life turn to them because they reflect every kind of mood that human life brings. In this book the author looks at twelve psalms reflecting twelve problems which bring people to the edge of despair. The titles of the chapters in the book are:-

When You Feel God Has Forgotten You
When You Are Depressed
When You Lose A Sense Of Wonder
When You Are Looking For Answers
When You Just Cannot Find Happiness
When You Are Afraid
When You Are In Trouble
When You Are On The Edge Of Despair
When Tongues Hurt You
When You Are Building
When You Can't Sleep

Foreword by Professor Norman Nevin
Published by
Ambassador Productions Ltd.
At £3.50 plus 25 p post and packing.